Everything You Need to Know About

Dating and Relationships

Dating can be a fun and exciting experience, giving you a chance to get to know someone else—and yourself—better.

Everything You Need to Know About

Dating and Relationships

Erin M. Hovanec

Published in 2000 by The Rosen Publishing Group, Inc.
29 East 21st Street, New York, NY 10010

First Edition

Library of Congress Cataloging-in-Publication Data

Hovanec, Erin M.
   Everything you need to know about dating and relationships / Erin M. Hovanec.
      p. cm. — (The need to know library)
   Includes bibliographical references and index.
   ISBN 0-8239-3081-5
   1. Dating (Social customs). 2. Man-woman relationships. I. Title. II. Series.
HQ801.H798 2000
646.7'7—dc21

                                                 99-045574

Manufactured in the United States of America

Contents

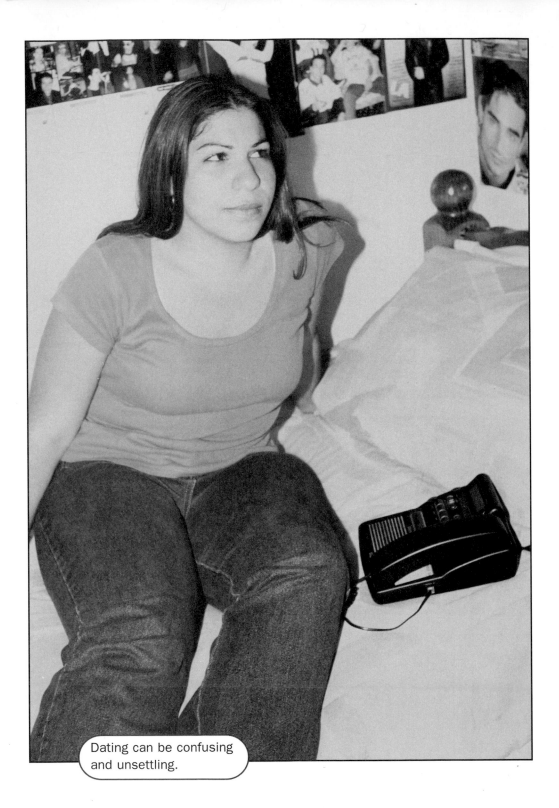

Dating can be confusing and unsettling.

Introduction

When Malik asked Anneta to go to a movie, she was so excited. She'd had a crush on Malik for what seemed like forever. Later, though, she started to get really nervous. "Do I have to choose the movie? What kind of movie should we see? What if he doesn't like it?" she wondered. "What will we talk about? Will he try to kiss me?"

Karl had been dating Sophia for almost six months. He thought things were going pretty well, but there was one problem. She didn't want to have sex. Sophia said that she liked Karl, but she just "wasn't ready." Karl didn't know what to do. "Does she really like me?" he wondered. "Should I just break up with her?"

Tallia and Matthew had been together since sophomore year. Everything was great between them, but, as seniors, they were worried about the future. Matthew was going to college in another state and didn't know if he could handle a long-distance relationship. What if Tallia met another guy? How often would he and Tallia be able to see each other if they lived in different cities?

It seemed as if all of Toni's friends had boyfriends. Hanging out with so many couples made Toni feel very left out. Toni had never even been on a date. She spent a lot of time working on the yearbook, and she was captain of the track team. "There must be something wrong with me," she thought. "I must be a loser."

Dating can be an exciting and fun experience. It gives you a chance to meet new people and try new things. While you are getting to know one another, you also get to know yourself. You can decide what is important to you and what is not so important, and learn about the kind of people you like and respect. Dating is a big part of growing up.

Dating can also be confusing and unsettling. There are a lot of choices and decisions to make, and you may not be sure of how to proceed. Maybe you have a crush on someone and don't know how to tell that person. Or maybe someone has a crush on you, and you aren't sure what to do. You may be afraid to ask someone on a date, or to go on a date if someone asks you. What will you talk about? Where will you go? Will you have to kiss? Will you want to have sex?

Dating is like riding a roller coaster. You want to try it, and you think you'll like it, but you aren't sure exactly what to expect. While it's happening, your stomach feels funny, your palms are sweaty, and you're scared to death. Then you suddenly realize that you are laughing, having fun, and enjoying yourself.

Dating—when you spend time with someone who you think of as more than a friend—can often lead to a romantic relationship. This experience is an exciting part of growing up. In such a relationship, you have to learn how to balance the time spent with your boyfriend or girlfriend with everything else in your life, such as school, friends, and family. You have to figure out when the right time is for you to get serious. You can talk about things such as dating exclusively (which means you go out only with each other and do not date other people), whether or not to have sex, and your future together. You might also have to figure out when a relationship isn't working, and if it is time to say goodbye.

While you are dating, just like riding a roller coaster, you also have to think about safety. You need to look out for yourself. That means learning about things such as date rape, birth control, sexually transmitted diseases (STDs), and physical and mental abuse. These things happen in all kinds of relationships, even between teenagers. You need to know how to be smart, stay safe, and get help if you need it.

Maybe you don't even want to date yet. Maybe your parents won't allow it. That's okay too. Every person is different, and different people start dating at different times. Some people do a lot of dating before they find someone with whom they want to have a relationship. Sometimes those relationships work, and other times they don't. Others find one person, date him or her, start a relationship, and live happily ever after.

When you are in a relationship, you learn about your values and your emotions. Honesty, trust, and respect are important aspects of any close friendship or relationship. And though dating and romantic relationships aren't always predictable or easy, they are enriching and are an important part of growing up.

Chapter One

To Date or Not to Date?

You may be asking yourself, "What does 'dating' mean, anyway?" The truth of the matter is that dating means many different things, depending on whom you talk to. How do you know if you are dating someone? Well, there isn't an easy answer to this question.

You can date someone you see every day or just once a week. You can also date someone who lives next door, across the country, or even across the world. You can date more than one person, or commit yourself to just one guy or girl. You may go out on dates to places like the movies or the local diner. If you don't drive, or don't have access to a car, you may just hang out together at school and at friends' house. And just because you are doing these things with someone doesn't always mean that you are dating. Maybe the two of you are just good friends.

People define dating in lots of ways. Take a look at the situations below.

Dunja and Jorge get together at least once a week. They tell each other almost everything, but they've never held hands, kissed, or referred to one another as "boyfriend" or "girlfriend."

Tyrone and Steph hang out with the same crowd. Twice, they've kissed at the end of the night.

Kyle and Leshona hooked up one night at a party. They were both drunk, and they ended up having sex. They've slept together a few times since then at parties, but they don't usually talk to each other at school.

Carlie and Marc have gone to the movies together a few times. Marc has been hanging out by Carlie's locker a lot lately. He just asked her to go to the prom with him.

Gregor and Lana have been a couple for two years. They've agreed not to date anyone else.

Which couples do you think are "dating"? Which ones are just hanging out together or being friends? These are tough questions to answer.

Confused? If you are, that's okay. Dating is complicated. The most important thing to remember is to talk to your partner. Make sure that you both agree on the kind of relationship you have. It is easy to hurt someone's feelings if you are not communicating clearly.

If you're not sure where you stand with someone, don't be afraid to ask him or her. Find out what kind of relationship the person thinks you two have, and what kind of relationship he or she wants to have with you in the future. Whether you decide to date or to be just friends, it is important to have an honest, open relationship and good communication.

How Do I Know If I'm Ready?

As a teenager, you are probably pretty curious about sex. Your body is changing, and you may be experiencing some emotions that are new to you. Suddenly, you may find yourself sexually attracted to others.

Along with these physical changes come many emotional changes. You may feel the need to try new things and be more independent. You may want to meet new people and start new relationships. Dating helps to teach you how to treat other people and also allows you to discover how you want to be treated by others. Through dating, you can grow as a person and become more confident, self-sufficient, and independent.

Some people begin dating in their early teens, whereas others wait until their twenties. Peer pressure—when people around you pressure you to do things that you wouldn't normally do—can be tough to deal with. Though it can be hard to stand up for what you believe in, ultimately, others will respect you for making your own choices. Don't let others make decisions for you. If you don't want to date now, do not let other people's opinions sway you. And if you do want to date, remember that in order for it to be a positive experience, you have to be mature enough to know what you want.

In any relationship, especially a romantic one, it is important to be sensitive. This means being able to respect someone else's thoughts, feelings, and opinions, regardless of whether or not you agree with him or her. You also should be able to communicate effectively with the person you date. You should be honest with each other and try to resolve your differences. Everyone feels hurt, jealous, and angry sometimes. Solving problems together makes a relationship stronger.

When you build a new relationship, you are also building trust. And with this bond should come comfort. If you are shy and nervous and find dating uncomfortable, maybe you should wait until you feel ready.

Does all of this sound hard to do? It is, but you don't need to do it all at once. People spend entire lifetimes learning to respect, trust, and communicate with the ones they care about. If you are willing to jump in and get started with all this, you are probably ready to date.

Parents? Not a Problem.

Your parents may want to be involved in your social life. If this is the case, and you have decided that you are ready to date, talk to your parents about your decision. It is better to be up-front, rather than sneaking around without their knowledge.

Explain why you feel ready to start dating. Presenting a thoughtful argument for dating will show them that you take it seriously and that you intend to behave responsibly. Your parents may put some restrictions on you, such as suggesting a curfew, or deciding how often you can date, where you are allowed to go, and if you can use the car. By showing your parents that you acknowledge their concerns, you will earn their trust.

Sometimes parents decide that teens should not date. Depending on your age, religion, and background, your parents may have certain ideas about when dating is appropriate. If your parents forbid you to date, ask them why. Perhaps you can address their concerns. If not, it is best to obey them. Disobeying your parents will cause them to lose trust in you and to doubt your maturity. If they do not want you to

Talk to your parents about using the car on dates.

date, wait a few months and then discuss dating with them again. Your responsible behavior may convince them that you are ready to date after all.

Chapter Two | Crushes, Flirts, and Other Scary Things

Shan had never liked history class. But this semester, history was his favorite class—because Tara was in it. Tara was this really hot girl Shan had noticed the first day of class. Whenever Tara looked at him, though, Shan felt his stomach drop and his face start to get red. He had never even spoken to her—he was afraid to. What would he say? Shan didn't think Tara even knew he existed.

It always happens when you least expect it. There you are, minding your own business, and you look up and see Him. Or maybe you're hanging out with your friends, and suddenly She walks by. Time stops, and the world around you fades away. That's it   you have a crush.

Crushes

When you have a crush, meaning that you like someone from afar, you usually want to get to know the object of your affection better. However, you may not be sure of how to go about this. Both guys and girls get crushes. Even adults have crushes. Sometimes teens have crushes on people who are much older than they are, such as a teacher, coach, or friend's mom or dad.

Crushes are fun, but they are scary too. The uncertainty about what to do about your crush can be exciting. As long as you do not become too obsessed, crushes are a safe way to get used to all the feelings that attraction brings. You may be tongue-tied and terrified around your crush. That's okay; he or she will never know. That is why crushes are fun. If you do start to date, you will experience some of the same feelings you had during your crush. This is good because you will be able to recognize the feelings that you are having, and they will not seem so strange.

Same-Sex Crushes

Many people have crushes on someone of the same sex. Girls can get crushes on other girls, and guys can get crushes on other guys. Teens often wonder if having a same-sex crush means that they are gay. Almost everyone has a same-sex crush during his or her life, and it is perfectly normal. We get crushes on people we like, admire, and respect, and we want them to like, admire, and respect us. Often same-sex crushes don't have an element of sexual or romantic attraction.

If you do feel sexually or romantically attracted to someone of the same sex, you might be gay. There's nothing wrong with being gay; it's just another way of loving and caring for others. Being gay means having a different kind of lifestyle from most people, but it's a perfectly normal one.

However, some people think that being gay is wrong or immoral, which can make things hard for gay teens. If you think you are gay, talk about it with someone you trust. He or she can encourage you and help you to find out more about services that support gay people.

Flirting: Do or Don't?

Stephanie had a huge crush on Keith. She wanted to get him to notice her, but she wasn't sure what to say to him. It seemed as though some girls just knew how to talk to guys, but Stephanie had never been good at flirting.

Stephanie knew Keith played basketball on the high school team; maybe they could talk about that. The problem was, she didn't really know anything about basketball. Should she fake it? Or maybe she could ask him a question about it. After all, he was the expert. But she didn't want him to think she was totally stupid about sports either.

When you have a crush on someone, you want that person to notice you. You want him or her to see that you are smart, funny, attractive, likable, and a good person. Basically, you want your crush to like you as much as you like him or her.

One way to get your crush to notice you—and hopefully like you—is to flirt. Flirting is acting in a way that draws attention to you and is often a playful way of getting to know someone. It is often associated with girls, but boys flirt, too.

Flirting often gets a bad rap, but it's not necessarily a negative thing. Flirting is a way of subtly expressing your attraction for someone. It's a great way to make a good impression on your crush.

The most important thing to remember while flirting is to be yourself. It is okay to show off all the good qualities you have, but don't go overboard. Good flirting is showing yourself to your best advantage. Bad flirting is pretending to be someone you're not. If you act less intelligent, capable, sensitive, or thoughtful than you really are, you're not showing your crush the real you. When it comes to flirting, it can be hard to know where to draw the line. Just be yourself. You are smart, talented, attractive, and fun—there's no need to act differently.

Okay, so you've decided that you are ready to date, and your parents approve. You have found the guy or girl that you would like to get to know better. You have

When flirting, act natural—don't go overboard.

made the first step in getting to know your crush. Maybe you have tried flirting, maybe not. Are you ready for the next big step—the date itself?

Chapter Three

Getting Started: Making a Date

Rob really liked Kristin. He wanted to ask her out but didn't know how. Should he just ask her if she wanted to hang out sometime? Or should he ask her to go somewhere, like to a movie or a restaurant or something? He also didn't want to ask her in front of anyone, but it seemed as though she was always with her friends. What if she said no? He would feel like a complete loser.

Just like writing a term paper, the hardest part of dating is getting started. Many teens say they don't date because they are afraid to ask someone out. Years ago, it was mainly guys who asked women for a date.

Today, however, girls are taking charge and asking guys out, too.

If you want to ask someone out, it may be easier if you plan in advance what you are going to say. Have an idea of where you would like to go on the date. Ask your date to do something specific, like go to a movie, a school dance, or a party. You will also want to speak to the person alone. Asking for a date is hard enough without a group of snickering guys or giggling females peering over your shoulder.

Let's be real—it is hard to ask someone out on a date. You are making yourself vulnerable and risking rejection. After all, the person could say no. But he or she could say yes, too! The best advice: Get up your courage, take a deep breath, and ask.

When the Risk Pays Off

You've taken a chance and asked. And the person said yes! Or maybe someone has asked you for a date. Now what? Whether you have been asked out or you've done the asking yourself, you'll want to be part of planning the date.

First dates don't have to be elaborate, expensive events. You can do something as simple and inexpensive as going to a friend's party or meeting at a school football game. The important thing is that you both agree on what to do.

If you have asked someone to go to a movie, find out what kind of films the person likes and then decide on

Dating in groups can make conversation much easier.

a film together. If someone has asked you to dinner, don't be shy about sharing your likes and dislikes. If you are a vegetarian, do not agree to go to a steakhouse. If you hate seafood and your date suggests going to a restaurant that specializes in fish dishes, speak up. Do not be afraid of hurting the other person's feelings. After all, if you don't enjoy the movie or the meal, you won't have a good time.

Consider planning your first date with a group of people. It makes conversation a lot easier, and the date may go more smoothly with others around. Dating in a group takes the pressure off of you and your date. You can go on a double date with another couple or just hang out with a bunch of friends. Rent a video together, hang out in the park, or pick another group activity. It's easier to be yourself when you are around people you are familiar with.

After picking the event together, decide on a time. Do you want to see a movie at night or an afternoon matinee? On a school night or a weekend? You will also need to think about transportation. Who is going to drive? If neither of you is old enough to drive, you'll have to arrange a way to get there and back or make a plan to meet. When planning your date, keep your parents' rules in mind. After all, you don't want to break curfew or borrow the car without asking and end up grounded.

Dealing with Rejection

Carlos was shocked when Amanda invited him to come over to her house and watch a movie. It wasn't as if she was having a bunch of people over. She was asking him on a date.

Carlos thought Amanda was nice, but he had never thought of her in a romantic way. Besides, he was thinking about asking out a girl in his algebra class. Carlos didn't want to hurt Amanda's feelings, but he didn't really want to go out with her.

Unfortunately, your crush may say no to a date. Dating disappointments happen to everyone, but they hurt just the same. If someone turns you down for a date, it is best to simply agree and walk away. People have all sorts of reasons for not going on a date, and often those reasons have nothing to do with you. Maybe that person isn't allowed to date, or maybe he or she already has a boyfriend or girlfriend. Sometimes a person simply isn't interested in you romantically.

If you question the girl in your chemistry class about why she turned you down for a date, you are likely to end up with hurt feelings. If she is trying to be considerate, don't make her explain in detail why she can't or doesn't want to go out with you. Also, don't argue. You

If you don't want to date someone, politely say no.

There is no rule about kissing on the first date!

won't change her mind, and you will both end up feeling very uncomfortable.

What if someone asks you out on a date and you don't want to go? It's perfectly acceptable to say no, and it's the best thing to do. Dating someone because you don't want to say no or because you feel bad for that person isn't fair to either of you. By accepting the date, you would be giving that person the impression that you are romantically interested when you aren't. Instead, be polite and say, "No, thanks."

Don't make excuses for saying no, unless they're true. If you tell Mike that you can't go out with him on Saturday night because you are cleaning your room, Mike might assume that you would go if you were not busy and will probably ask you out again. What will you say then? A firm, polite "No, thank you" will let Mike down gently without giving him false hope.

The Big Moment

A word about kissing: Despite what some people say, there is no rule about kissing on the first date. Do what feels right for you. If you like the person, and you want to kiss him or her, go ahead. If you don't feel ready yet, you don't have to kiss anyone. And don't be insulted if your date doesn't try to kiss you. If the time is right, the kiss will happen.

Chapter Four

What Is a Relationship, Anyway?

Erica was nervous when Nick invited her to his house for dinner. She had never met his parents. But Nick told her not to worry. He said that they had always been nice to his girlfriends.

"Girlfriend? Is that what I am?" she thought. She and Nick had been hanging out a lot for the past few weeks, but they had never talked about their relationship. "Does this mean that he's my boyfriend?" she wondered. "And what does THAT mean?"

We all have many different kinds of relationships. You have relationships with parents, brothers and/or sisters, and other relatives. You also have relationships with friends, acquaintances, peers, coworkers, team members, and teachers. But when we talk about a "relationship" here, it refers to a romantic relationship between two people who care for each other.

After two people have gone on a few dates, they usually realize that they are getting to know one another better. At this stage, a relationship is starting to develop. In a relationship, you can learn more about your partner's likes and dislikes, family and friends, hopes, dreams, fears, and sense of humor.

However, in any relationship in which you share your innermost thoughts and feelings, you are also vulnerable, meaning that you are at risk of getting hurt. You are sharing private parts of yourself with someone. A relationship can be scary, but it can also be wonderful. Being part of a healthy relationship can teach you a lot about yourself.

The Right Stuff

Boyfriends and girlfriends have all sorts of ways of relating to and behaving with each other. You may know some couples who are very serious and others who joke around a lot. Maybe you know some couples who spend lots of time together, whereas other couples see each other only once in a while. Different people have different ways of being together, but a few elements are key to all healthy relationships.

Couples in healthy relationships make communication a priority.

Communication

In a healthy relationship, couples talk openly to one another. They share with each other their thoughts, opinions, emotions, and ideas. Couples even tell each other when they feel hurt, angry, ashamed, or jealous. It is not always easy to share your feelings with someone else, but it is very important. By revealing more about yourselves, you get to know each other better. By sharing your problems, hurts, and frustrations, you can then figure out a way to resolve them together. That makes your relationship stronger.

Individuality

It is important to be comfortable with who you are, especially when you are in a relationship. Each person brings something unique and special to the relationship. Couples complement one another by playing off each other's strengths and weaknesses. Think about the qualities or character traits that you like best about your girlfriend or boyfriend.

Honesty and Trust

Honesty builds trust, and trust is an essential part of a happy relationship. Couples need to be truthful with each other and up-front about problems and other complicated issues. As a couple, you rely on each other. It is important that you and your partner trust each other and believe that the other will be there for emotional support in times of need.

Respect

To show respect means that you value the opinions, beliefs, and ideas of someone else. Basically, you believe in that person. People in healthy relationships respect one another. They do not purposely hurt, put down, or upset each other. Though they may not always see eye-to-eye about everything, they respect their partner's opinion.

Keeping It in Perspective

Colin and Maggie have been dating for over a year; they are inseparable. They meet at Maggie's locker before school each day, eat lunch together, and then hung out after school.

33

Until Colin quit the baseball team, he and Maggie had not seen a lot of each other. Between all the practices and games, he didn't have much free time. Afterward, things were better. Maggie's friends complain that they never see her anymore, but she tries to make them understand. After all, she's in love.

It's easy to get wrapped up in a relationship when you think that you have found the perfect girl or guy. You are getting to know each other better and having a great time. It sometimes seems as if nothing is as much fun as being with your boyfriend or girlfriend. However, it is important to keep things in perspective. You need to find a balance between your relationship and all the other aspects of your life. These include your family, friends, school, a part-time job, pets, hobbies, and other interests.

Before you get too caught up in a new relationship, take a moment to think about what makes you unique. What are your talents and your strengths? Are you a musician, a writer, an athlete, or just an all-around fun, interesting person? Do not neglect the rest of your life. You will need to learn how to balance your responsibilities.

Your talents and hobbies make you happy, so do not stop pursuing them. Also, you should be careful not to neglect the people who care about you. With your family and good friends by your side, providing comfort and support, you can probably make it through anything.

You don't need to spend all of your time with your boyfriend or girlfriend in order for your relationship to strong. The more you do and learn individually, the more you will have to contribute to your relationship. People who truly care about you want you to be the best, most talented, and most interesting person you can be.

Chapter Five | Dating Smarts and Safety

Dating and relationships are an important part of growing up—something that many teens want to experience. However, there are some concerns that you should be aware of with regard to dating and relationship safety. If you want to make the most of your teen years, you need to be smart and stay safe.

Date and Acquaintance Rape

Joachim had invited Maria to his house to watch a movie. His parents were out, so they had the place to themselves. They had just begun to watch the movie when Joachim started kissing Maria. He pulled open her shirt and tried to unbutton

The word "no" should *always* be respected.

her jeans. Maria kept pushing his hand away, but Joachim kept moving it back.

Finally Maria got angry. "If you didn't want to watch the movie, why did you even invite me over?" she asked furiously.

"You know why," Joachim shouted. "You've been teasing me for the last two months. Now that we're finally alone, you suddenly change your mind. How dumb do you think I am?"

Joachim tried to shove Maria back down on the couch. Maria was terrified that Joachim would hurt her, but she pushed him off of her, quickly grabbed her coat, and fled from the house.

Date rape occurs when two people are on a date and one person forces the other to have sex. Acquaintance rape means that the rapist is someone the victim knows but is not necessarily dating. Both guys and girls can be date rapists, and both guys and girls can be the victims. However, in most date rape situations, females are the victims and males are the aggressors.

Because they are less sexually experienced, teens are particularly vulnerable to date rape and acquaintance rape. According to the United States Department of Health and Human Services, more than twenty percent of sexually active girls age fifteen and under said that their first experience of sexual intercourse was forced on them.

Some date rapists are violent criminals who threaten to hurt or kill their victims. More often, most date rapists are males who force women to have sex by pressuring and physically intimidating them. For both people involved in a relationship, regardless of whether they are male or female, it is extremely important to be sensitive to what your partner wants. If your date or partner says that he or she does not want to have sex, respect that choice. Try not to put sexual pressure on your partner. Instead, talk about what you both want and try to figure out a way to meet each other's needs.

It is especially important for women to be very clear about their sexual choices. If you don't want to have sex, tell your date "no" firmly. If he persists, leave or call for help. Also, you are allowed to change your mind, even at the last minute. Maybe you thought you wanted to have sex, but then you realized you didn't. Sex is not something you should engage in because you feel guilty. You can always say no—no matter what. And remember, rape is never your fault.

Dating Smarts

To stay safe, you'll need to be cautious on dates, especially when you don't know the person well. By following the tips below, you can avoid many dangerous situations.

- Avoid being alone with someone you don't know well or trust completely.

- Drive yourself to and from a date or arrange transportation beforehand. Don't get into a car alone with someone you don't know well.

- Always bring money on a date in case you need to call someone to pick you up or pay for transportation home.

- Don't drink alcohol or take drugs and don't stay with a date who does. People under the influence of alcohol and drugs make poor decisions.

- If your date seems angry, violent, abusive, or unstable, leave immediately.

- Trust your instincts. If you feel uncomfortable or frightened, call for help or get out of the situation immediately.

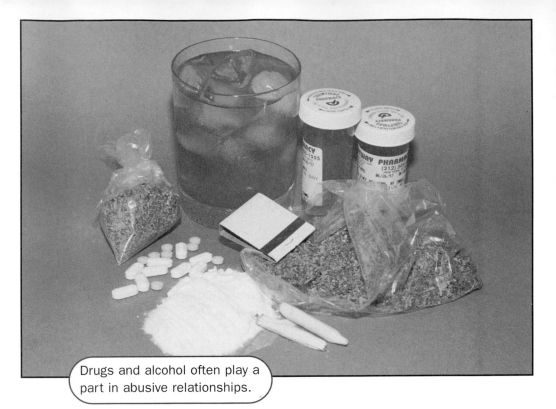

Drugs and alcohol often play a part in abusive relationships.

Recognizing an Abusive Relationship

Whenever they argue, Juanita's boyfriend gets uncontrollably angry. He shoves her, shakes her, and once he even slapped her.

Colleen has told Mark-Luke over and over that she doesn't want to have sex. Whenever they're making out, he grabs her breasts and tries to pull off her clothes. It's only when she starts crying that he finally stops.

Connor's girlfriend makes fun of him whenever he makes a mistake. She calls him a "moron," a "loser," "stupid," or "worthless."

More than 70,000 women are assaulted each year; more than two-thirds of them are under age eighteen. Also, approximately one of every three high school students—both male and female—is or has been involved in an abusive relationship. Teens who plan to date need to know the signs of an abusive relationship.

An abusive relationship is one in which one person mistreats the other in some way. The abuse can be physical, sexual, or emotional. Abusers often have other problems in their lives. They may have emotional problems, drug or alcohol problems, or difficulties at home. Even so, there is no excuse for abuse. Hurting someone is definitely not the right way to deal with your own problems and frustrations. Similarly, if someone has abused you in any way, it is not your fault. No one asks to be hurt, and no one deserves it. You need to get away from your abuser and get help.

Help Is Out There

If you have been raped or abused, you need to get help right away. You may feel as though you are all alone, but you aren't. Many people have experienced date or acquaintance rape and have survived. All sorts of resources are available to help you. First of all, you need to get to a safe place away from your attacker or abuser. Tell a parent, friend, teacher, or someone else you trust what has happened. He or she can encourage and support you while you get help.

If you have been raped or abused, don't go it alone.

If you've been raped or physically or sexually abused, call the police and get medical attention. Eventually you'll have to tell your parents. Remember, you have done nothing wrong. There is no reason to feel guilty or ashamed. If you think you will have trouble telling your parents, ask someone to be there with you to help you.

People who have been raped or abused have to cope with feelings such as anger, shame, embarrassment, depression, and sometimes even thoughts of suicide. Talking about what you are feeling is the best way to handle your emotions. You can speak to a guidance counselor, therapist, or someone else you think can help you to get through this. Many people have survived rape and abuse; you can, too.

Chapter Six

Getting Serious: Beyond Dating

Brian had been dating Emily for almost six months. They spent a lot of time together, and neither of them wanted to go out with anyone else. They decided not to date anyone except each other. Brian and Emily really cared about each other, and they knew that this was the right choice for them.

Just the Two of You

After you have been dating the same person for a while, there may come a time when you discover that your relationship is getting more serious. The two of you are probably spending more time together, you tell each other things you would not tell other people, and you are growing closer emotionally. When this happens, you may decide that you want to date only each other. If you decide to date one person exclusively, this means that you and your partner agree that neither of you will date anyone else. Some couples even exchange small gifts as a sign of their commitment.

Going steady with someone takes your relationship to a new level. It requires even more trust, honesty, and communication. It also requires sacrifice, because each of you is giving up the opportunity to date other people. Before you agree to date someone exclusively, think about how that will change your social life. If you don't think you are ready or think you may get bored or restless dating only one person, you may want to wait.

On the other hand, if you think you are ready to commit to one person, go ahead and do it. Dating exclusively is an important part of learning about yourself and can show you what you need to be in a relationship. It teaches you a lot about the qualities of a healthy and beneficial relationship. You learn a lot about caring for and loving another person.

What About Sex?

Lately, Steve had been pressuring Garcia to have sex. He was her first boyfriend, and she didn't want to lose him. But she also didn't know if she was ready for sex. It seemed like all of Garcia's friends were having sex. She sometimes felt like a little kid around them.

Steve said sex would make them closer, and that she would finally be a woman. Garcia wasn't sure if that was true. What if they had sex and then broke up? Or worse, what if she got pregnant? She wanted to act like an adult, but she sure wasn't ready for a baby.

Sex is a normal part of a healthy, committed relationship between two mature people. Sex requires maturity and responsibility. If you are thinking about having sex, you will want to give some thought to how sex will change your relationship. You may feel as though everyone but you is having sex, but that is not true. Actually, in North America, the number of teens waiting to have sex until they are in a committed, adult relationship is rising.

If you decide to have sex, you will also want to think about the possible consequences. Sex can result in a sexually transmitted disease (STD) or pregnancy. You should both see a doctor before having sex to make sure that you are not carrying any STDs. Even if you haven't had sex, you could still be infected with an STD. If you have had sex, especially unprotected sex, you are at high risk. According to the Centers for Disease Control, every year in the United States about one of four sexually active teens contract a sexually transmitted disease. Also, what would you do if you found out that you were going to become a parent? How would you deal with the pregnancy? You and your partner should discuss the possibility of disease and pregnancy before you have sex.

Do you feel as though you can discuss these things with your partner? Are you uncomfortable or embarrassed? If so, then you may not be ready for sex. If you are embarrassed to talk about the possibility of pregnancy, how will you deal with it if it happens? If you are not yet mature enough to discuss sex, then you are not yet mature enough to have it.

Staying Safe

If you and your partner do decide that you are ready to have sex, you will want to take precautions against STDs and pregnancy. The male should always wear a condom. It protects against both STDs and pregnancy.

You should also use a second method to protect against pregnancy; condoms are not one hundred percent effective. According to the Alan Guttmacher Institute, one million teens become pregnant in the United States every year. There are many ways to prevent or decrease your chances of becoming pregnant. However, the only sure way to prevent pregnancy is not to have sex.

Some other common kinds of birth control include birth control pills and diaphragms. Together you and

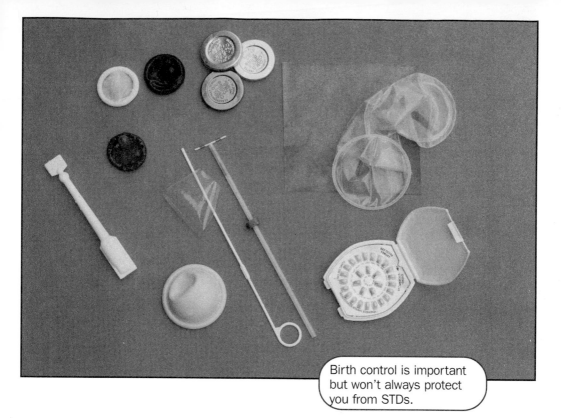

Birth control is important but won't always protect you from STDs.

your partner should decide what kind of birth control you will use. Also, both of you should be aware of how your chosen method of birth control works. Birth control is the responsibility of both partners in a relationship. It's not simply a "man's problem" or a "woman's problem." If you are old enough to have sex, you're also old enough to do it safely and responsibly.

The Future

As you get older, you will need to think about what role your relationship will play in your future. When you near the end of high school, you will start considering new options—going to college, getting a job, or possibly moving to a new place.

Across the Miles: Long-Distance Relationships

If you or your partner are moving away after high school, you will have to decide if you want to continue your relationship. You can have a "long-distance" relationship, in which you are still together but don't see each other as often as you would if you lived nearby. You might only see each other twice a month, once a month, or maybe even only once every few months. Long-distance relationships can be just as happy and healthy as those in which people see each other every day. However, they require an added level of commitment.

Some people decide to stay together even if they are separated by many miles, and their relationships are stronger because of it. Others decide that they can't handle a long-distance relationship. They think they will be lonely or feel left out if they aren't dating someone who lives nearby. Talk to your partner and together decide what is right for you.

A Lifetime Commitment

Some young people are so committed to each other that they decide to get married. Marriage is a huge decision—one that you should consider very carefully. When you get married, you are committing yourself to another person for the rest of your life. You are saying, "This person is the one for me. I don't need to date anymore or try out any more new relationships. I've found my lifetime partner."

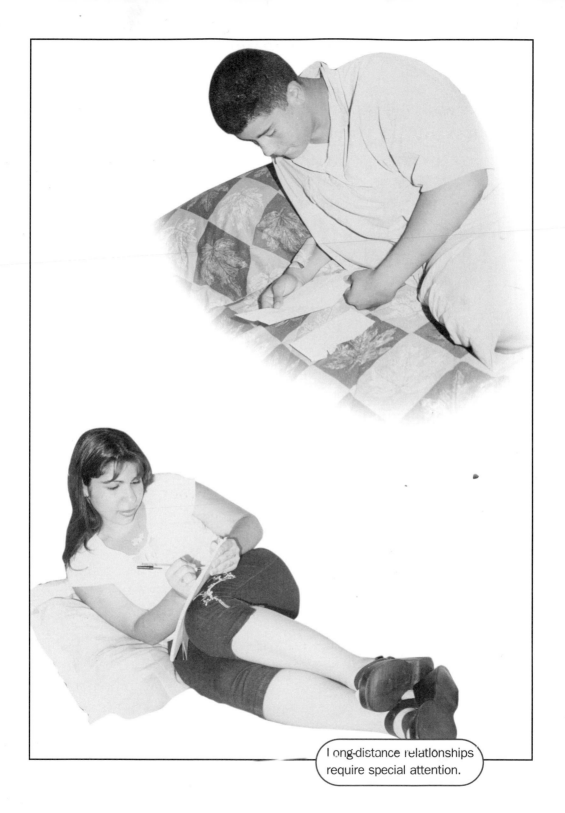

Long-distance relationships require special attention.

Unfortunately, the majority of teenage marriages end in divorce. As you get older, you will grow and change in many ways. You are still developing your adult identity in your twenties and even your thirties. Your likes and dislikes, opinions and interests—all these can change radically. The person you thought you wanted to be with forever when you were seventeen might not be the person you want to be with when you are twenty-five years old.

If you are truly in love with someone, that love will last. Consider waiting a few years before getting married. You don't need to hurry into any big decisions. If you are right for each other, your love won't fade. By waiting to marry, you will give your relationship time to develop and grow. Then, when you're ready to say "I do," it will mean even more.

Chapter Seven | When It's Over: Breaking Up

Going on dates and being in a relationship helps you to discover what kind of person you feel the most comfortable with. By dating different people, you can see what sort of person fits you best. You will also realize what sort of person you don't want as a partner and discover who isn't right for you. Relationships are learning experiences—even the ones that do not work out the way that you would have liked. All relationships help you figure out what you don't want in life.

If you don't have fun with your guy or girl anymore—if you argue a lot or seem to have grown far apart—it may be time to reassess your relationship. Analyze the feelings you have for your partner. Does he add something special to your life? Does she make you happy? If you have tried to work things out but you are still not happy, that means that it's time to break up.

Letting Someone Down Easy

When Martha and Adam first started dating, things were great. But after a few months, Martha started to become bored. She felt like she was spending too much time with Adam. She missed hanging out with her friends and having time to herself.

Martha tried to explain the way she felt to Adam, but he didn't understand. He said that if Martha really liked him, she would want to be with him. Martha just couldn't make him see her side. Finally, she gave up; they were too different for things to work out. She decided it was time to break up, but she didn't know how to tell Adam.

When you are in a relationship with someone, it is because you care about him or her. Most of the time, even if you want to end a relationship, you probably will still care for your boyfriend or girlfriend and do not want to hurt him or her. It can be difficult to end a relationship in a nonhurtful way. It takes a lot of maturity.

It might be tempting to try to force the relationship to end so that you won't have to actually break up. You may find yourself treating your boyfriend or girlfriend badly or doing things to push him or her away. Often you may not realize that you are behaving this way. You may think that if you are inconsiderate enough or mean enough, it will force your boyfriend or girlfriend to break up with you. This plan might work, but you will both feel hurt and angry in the end. Besides, you probably do not really want to mistreat someone you care about. You owe it to your guy or girl to be honest.

When you decide it is time to break up, pick a private place to tell the person. Tell him or her how you feel, and why you think it is best for you to end your relationship. Be honest, but don't hurt the person unnecessarily. Be prepared for him or her to ask questions. You also owe it to the person to explain why you are breaking up.

Don't be surprised if he or she gets upset. After you have finished explaining yourself, leave the person alone to deal with the news. It might take a while for it to sink in, and he or she will probably want some space in order to be able to figure things out on his or her own. However, if the person seems extremely upset and you think that your boyfriend or girlfriend might hurt himself or herself, stay with the person until someone else arrives.

Dealing with Getting Dumped

When Martha told him she wanted to break up, Adam was shocked. He thought that things were going great between them. She explained how she felt, and she was really nice about it, but Adam still felt terrible. He knew Martha wouldn't change

*her mind. How was he going to face her in school?
And what would his friends say? Everyone was
going to think he was a total loser.*

While it is hard to break up with someone, it is even harder to have someone break up with you. People call this "getting dumped" because that is often how it feels. No matter how you think a relationship is going, people rarely expect the breakup when it happens. If someone ends a relationship with you, you need to accept that it is over. The reality of the end of your relationship may take a while to sink in, but you have to respect the other person's decision. Trying to change his mind or win her back will only make things more stressful and uncomfortable for both of you.

If someone breaks up with you, take some time alone to think about the relationship and to figure out how to deal with your feelings. You might see that the decision is the best one for you, too. Or maybe that will take some time. This is a good time to turn to your friends. Everyone, no matter how popular or attractive, has been dumped. Your friends will understand how you feel and will be able to comfort you.

It also helps to keep busy. Remind yourself that you have a very full life, even without the relationship. Remember that you had a great life before you began the relationship. Things can be even better after it's over.

If you truly feel devastated by the breakup, you may

A romantic breakup can be extremely painful.

want to seek help. Being dumped can make you feel hurt, lonely, depressed and sad. However, if your feelings are too powerful to handle or last well after the relationship has ended, talk to your parents, a teacher, or a guidance counselor, and tell this person how you are feeling. They can assist you in finding a professional counselor who can help you to handle your feelings.

Moving On

When a relationship ends, it sometimes feels like the end of the world. It takes some time to recover from the hurt and loneliness that comes with a breakup. This is true even when you are the person who ends the relationship.

Remember that being single and on your own has lots of advantages. Now is your chance to enjoy it. You can spend time with friends you lost touch with and reconnect with your family. You can get that perfect 4.0 GPA you have been after, or try something you've never done before. Take a kickboxing class. Read a really good novel. Start writing in a journal so that you can record your feelings and look back at this time later on. Suddenly you will find that you have a lot more free time. Do something fun with it.

Spending time with good friends can help you to get over any breakup!

Glossary

abusive relationship Relationship in which one or both people abuse the other physically, sexually, or emotionally.

acquaintance rape When someone you know forces you to have sex against your will.

breakup The end of a relationship.

crush Strong romantic attraction to someone who is not aware of your feelings.

date Social engagement between two people who are usually interested in each other romantically.

date rape When a date forces you to have sex against your will.

depressed To feel extremely sad; to be uninterested in your life and your environment.

exclusive Only one.

flirt To act in a way that draws attention to you and makes you seem attractive.

gay Sexually or romantically attracted to someone of the same sex.

individuality Traits that make a person unique and special.

peer pressure When people your age, often friends or classmates, pressure you to do something that you wouldn't normally do

rejection Feeling unloved or unwanted.

Where to Go for Help

In the United States

Domestic Violence Hotline
(800) 621-HOPE

Planned Parenthood Federation of America
810 Seventh Ave
New York, NY 10003
(800) 223-3303
(212) 541-7800
Web site: http://www.plannedparenthood.org

Rape, Abuse, and Incest National Network (RAINN)
635-B Pennsylvania Avenue
Washington, DC 20003
(800) 656-HOPE
Web site: http://www.rainn.org
e-mail: RAINNmail@aol.com

Sexuality Information and Education Council of the
   United States (SIECUS)
130 West 42nd Street, Suite 350
New York, NY 10036
(212) 819-9770
Web site: http://www.siecus.org

Smart Date
P.O. Box 13232
San Luis Obispo, CA 93406
(805) 546-4941
Web site: http://www.smartdate.com
e-mail: info@smartdate.com

In Canada

Ottawa Sexual Assault Centre Hotline
(613) 234-2266

Planned Parenthood Federation of Canada
1 Nicholas Street, Suite 430
Ottawa, Ontario K1N 7B7
(613) 241 4474
Web site: http://www.ppfc.ca/
e-mail: admin@ppfc.ca

Teen Help Line
(800) 668-6868

For Further Reading

Bell, Ruth. *Changing Bodies, Changing Lives: A Book for Teens on Sex and Relationships.* New York: Times Books, 1998.

Levy, Barrie. *In Love and in Danger: A Teen's Guide to Breaking Free of Abusive Relationships.* Seattle, WA: Seal Press, 1998.

McCoy, Kathy, et al. *The New Teenage Body Book.* New York: Perigee, 1992.

Moe, Barbara. *Everything You Need to Know About Sexual Abstinence.* New York: Rosen Publishing Group, 1998.

Mufson, Susan, and Rachel Kranz. *Straight Talk About Date Rape.* New York: Facts on File, 1997.

Pinsky, Drew, et al. *The Dr. Drew and Adam Book: A Survival Guide to Life and Love.* New York: Dell, 1998.

Index

About the Author

Erin M. Hovanec is a writer and editor living in New York City.

Photo Credits

Cover image & p. 48 by Thaddeus Harden, pp. 2, 6, 21, 24, 27, 48, 55 by Simca Israelian; p. 37 by Kim Sonsky, pp. 39, 41 by Ira Fox, p. 53 by Lauren Piperno, p. 16 © Corbis; p. 46 © The Image Works.

Design and Layout

Mike Caroleo